FROM THE HEART

FROM THE HEART

Poems of Praise and Thanks

Century Publishing
London Melbourne Auckland Johannesburg

CONTENTS

FROM THE HEART
Genevieve Noglik

I find myself unable to pray
To my Lord.
My mind is blank – I've nothing to say,
Though there should be something every day
To talk about with God.

Just repeating words is not for me,
It must come from the heart.
I truly hope that God can see
I don't know where to start.

At the wonderful things I marvel each day,
That God has made for man.
What else is there for me to say
But thank God all I can?

PRAISE YOU, FATHER
Marilyn Ashcroft

Praise You, Father, for sunshine,
Praise You, Father, for rain.
Praise You, Father, for good times,
Praise You, Father, for pain.

For if there was only sunshine
The flowers would never grow.
They need the refreshing rain,
They need the winds to blow.

If life was only good times,
Our faith would never grow.
God uses the times when we struggle
And when we are tossed to and fro.

So praise You, Father, whatever
You send upon life's way.
For You also send power to conquer
And a love that will always stay.

WORSHIP
Janet Gould

The world is a shrine to the Lord.
Blue-robed choir members
Flit from tree to tree
Delivering impromptu solos
In stereophonic praise.
The sun smiles warmly
On myriad altars
Golden-glossed with columbine.
A rabbit bounces down the aisle;
Lizards skitter and balance,
Skitter and balance;
The ants are on parade.
And all seems poured into
A warm blending
Of praise
And joy.

WERE YOU THERE?
Sister Maree CHN

Were You there where
The sea and sky met
And embraced each other?
Were You there
Where only the cry of the gulls
And the singing of the wind
Broke the deep silence?
Where shells like the
Jewels of kings shone in crystal pools,
Were You there?
I kicked the sand with my toes
And laughed at the sun
And knew You were there.

THE SUSSEX DOWNS
Angela Upton Cheney

Up here where mostly thorn and bramble-bush
Or the occasional neat hill-crest copse
Breaks surface, every passing cloud and gleam
Upon these slopes is like an artist's brush
Touching, retouching, where the landscape
   drops
And swells again, until they almost seem
To bend and ripple, hearing still perhaps
The wash and murmur of primordial surf
Lapping the shores of some long-vanished sea
Where now the plover rests, and silence wraps
Its spell about the aromatic turf
Masking these tideways of pre-history. . . .
While, overhead, against the wide bright arc
Above the ridge, where Earth with Heaven
   blends
On the blue confines of infinity,
Spills madly out the love song of the lark,
Floating until it finally descends,
Note by impassioned note, to here, and me . . . .

How good to think, when my last climb is done,
That someone else might pause where I do now,
Finding their peace beneath the Downland sky,
Sensing the magic of the Downland sun,
Loving it all from some great Downland brow:
Then would I never need to say goodbye!

GOD'S GEMS
J. Dalmain

Jasmine, pearl-white, against the sky,
Easter lilies with golden eye,
Winter berries, rich ruby red,
Evening stars in sapphire blue bed,
Laughing raindrops like diamonds fall –
Showering God's gems upon us all.

DAFFODILS
B.F. Burgess

Daffodils,
Golden as the rising sun,
Speak of spring ere winter's done,
Sing of hope and joy anew,
A love song from the world for me
And you.

Daffodils,
Fresh as the brook so clear,
Tell me what I need to hear,
Whispering secrets of summer days,
A song of love for all the world
To praise.

Daffodils,
Gentle as the summer breeze,
Raise our hearts to joys like these,
Herald of warm days yet to come,
A song of love to draw us all
Back home.

IF I COULD CHOOSE
Meryl Tookaram

If I could choose the time of
Day in which to live
I would choose dawn
With all the promise that
It brings.
The hushed quiet of the
Unawakened world,
The excitement of waiting
For the first bird call.
Grass, flowers, embraced
With heavy dew.
With the coming of dawn,
All life
Seems to be
Renewed.

THE DAWN CHORUS
Irene Hodgkinson

I'm waiting now, taut and still,
Hoping that very soon I will
Hear the first bird awake and trill.
Soon the air around will fill
With joyous songs from all until
My heart's so full that all I feel
Is an ecstasy so strong and real.
To feel uplifted in this way
Is a wonderful start to any day,
And as dawn breaks it seems to say
My happiness is here to stay.
Flowers start to open,
Trees start to sway.
Thank you, God, for my happiness
And another lovely day.

SPRING IN THE MOUNTAINS
Sister Michael Edgar

Spring is in the mountains,
A purple mist envelops
The mountain slopes and woodlands,
The air is full of sound.

The little streams are flowing
Over their mossy beds,
And wayside flowers, wet with dew,
Lift up their fragrant heads.

The mist is slowly rising
From each mountain's verdant breast,
A lark's song pours in rapture
As he soars out from his nest.

Ah, spring is in the mountains,
Yes, it has come again,
With peace and hope and gladness
To nature and to men.

SING A NEW SONG
Marilyn Ashcroft

Sing a new song to the Lord,
Praise and glorify His name,
He is the great unchanging,
He is evermore the same.

He is the rock of ages
And beneath His mighty shade
You can shelter from the storms of life
And never be afraid.

He is the Lord of Heaven and Earth
And His great creative hand
Formed the restless, surging seas
And the rich and fertile land.

He is our great salvation.
Let us with one accord
Join hearts and hands together
As we praise the living Lord.

YEARNINGS
Patricia Hadgifotis

Oh Lord my God,
I hear You in the gentle breeze,
Your passing through the swaying trees,
Your kiss I feel through restless leaves,
Caressing.
Peace fills my aching soul,
My silent heart's cry echoes Your own.

My heart rejoices in the Lord my God,
My soul yearns and sighs with love to Thee,
Returning from obscurity,
Fulfilled into eternity.

NIGHT
Sheelagh FitzGerald

Oh, walk with me to feel the peace
Of gentle dark and quiet lanes,
Where birds are still, and fox and badger roam.
The velvet softness, and that sense
Of sharing in nocturnal life.
It is when we escape man's world
Of care and noise
That we begin to know our soul,
Our very being . . . who we are
And why.
I tread softly, yet my footsteps sound,
Accenting every rustling leaf
Or snap of twig.
There is an awe, I feel, in this strange
World of night – intruding.
But I am close to You, God, and to Your
Wild creatures, who in their simplicity
Know You better than I.

I SING TO THE WIND
Sister Maree CHN

I sing to the wind as it plays on my face,
I laugh at the sky.
On a cloudless day, I touched the trunk of a
White gum.
Soft as a baby's cheek.
I kissed the flowers
And I danced with creation.
I tell the summer what great things
You have done.
Tell the winter of Your sufferings,
My tears like the stream flow for creation.
I cry that the land is dry and parched
Like the souls of men.
Shout to the fire of your power.
I whisper to the wild flowers of Your love,
And I sing and I dance with creation.
I tell Your happiness to the woods and
    mountains
And I mourn and grieve for Your lost.
Tell the cities of Your hope,
Tell mankind of Your love,
And I laugh and I dance with creation.

ON GOING TO CHURCH
J.M. Goldie

As you open the door
The peacefulness comes to meet you.
Welcomes you in,
Says, 'Rest awhile, refresh your soul,
Kneel and pray . . . .
And then, renewed,
Continue on your way.'

As you kneel there in peace
The sun, streaming in through the window,
Gilding your hair,
Lends you an aura, a halo.
Wait, be still.
In the silence
God will reveal His will.

As you rise to your feet,
Picking up all your belongings,
Your cares, returning,
Hustle you back to your duties,
Back to life.
Life abundant!
Triumphant over strife.

As you go forth to meet
The sun, the world and life,
Hold your head high.
The halo there may rest,
And, shining forth,
Inspire you on,
That you may do your best.

SHARED PRAYERS
Janet Gould

If I could share an attitude
Of thankfulness today,
I'd give the gift of gratitude:
Shared prayers
Among the multitude.

RAINDROPS
Maud Poulton

The rain has ceased, and after the shower
There is left upon each lovely flower,
Or so 'twould seem,
A precious gem. As such the raindrops shine,
To the blooms which hold them
   they are as wine.
Perchance I dream!

No matter! Nectar sweet and jewels rare,
These are nature's own, and none can compare
God's gifts to earth.
I like to think that these the real things are,
And not the products of man, valued far
Above their worth.

OUR HOME
Glenda Mitchel Palmer

This earthly home is cosy warm
With sunbeams from on high,
And cools its face with deep blue lakes
And showers' gentle sigh.

The sturdy redwoods form the frame,
The starry sky, the tent;
Nailed down with waves and waterfalls,
Crisp breezes – window vents.

Rich velvet clover covers floors:
A carpet, emerald, soft;
And smooth cold boulder mountain tops:
Majestic scenes aloft.

Appreciation of God's gifts
Put on this planet now;
Mere glimpses of our heavenly home . . .
Before His throne, I bow.

A PRAYER
Genevieve Noglik

Lord, when You take me from this life,
Please don't prolong the final strife,
Just take me quickly up above
And welcome me with all Your love.

Don't let me lie for weeks on end,
So helpless and without a friend,
Or in a home just left to die
With nothing but to dream and sigh.

I only want to be a whole,
My faculties all in control.
Don't let me linger on . . . and on
While most my age have passed and gone.

Don't leave my body and take my mind,
Or leave me deaf and almost blind.
I'd like to keep my sense and sight
To savour to the last . . . delight.

Alas, I fear I am too bold
To ask so much when not yet old.
I should embrace each day you give,
And thank You, Lord – for I do live!

MY CROWN
Glenda Mitchel Palmer

As my crown will be in Heaven,

May I take the gifts
You have given me on earth
And use them
To your glory;

Returning them to You
Not quite the same,
Because they go back
With all my love.

REVELATION REMEMBERED
Myra Reeves

If nevermore His face I see
In pure light pouring into me,
And if I may not feel again
The splendour of this quickening pain,
Nor break in glory as I pray –
I thank Thee, Lord, for this good day.

No morning ever woke so fair,
A singing radiance lit the air,
The mistle-thrush on pear tree top,
Outburst in song no storm could stop.
The house was filled with light more rare
Than ever sunshine scattered there.

And as I swept the dining room,
The Holy Spirit blessed my broom
And lit upon my hands, I think,
Nor left me at the kitchen sink.
The streets were filled with shining folk,
I loved them as they smiled and spoke.

My hands and hair were dripping flowers,
I could have walked the world for hours,
A lovelier sky I had not seen,
Its blue was washed and cherub-clean.
And all that had been pain was lost,
In glory of the Holy Ghost.

The quiet church drew like a spell,
In rapture on my knees I fell,
And lifted up my soul in prayer –
And straightway Jesus Lord was there.
More lovely than remembered bliss,
No earthly beauty white as His.

And joy to feel such grace again,
Evoked intolerable pain.
Till all my tears had found release,
In God's illimitable peace.
And this I pray . . . and this I pray,
That when my sweet strength ebbs away,
I shall remember this good day.

WANDERLIED
Sister Michael Edgar

Give me the open spaces,
The rough wind on my cheek,
Cries of the mating wild birds,
Through silences that speak.
Give me the white road's winding
Under a noonday sun,
Hush of a starlit Heaven,
And rest when day is done.

Give me the paths of freedom,
The far horizon's call,
Where the blue mountains beckon,
And silver waters fall.
And grant me strength of purpose,
Where'er the road may wend,
To find, beyond the striving,
Peace at the long day's end.

MOTHER
Thomas Foy

Just a little verse to greet you,
Dearest Mother, kindest friend.
Just a word to say I love you,
And will love you till life's end.

Mother dear, I am so grateful
For the lessons you have taught,
For your gentle words of wisdom
When your kindly help I sought.

Mother dear, my thoughts are with you
On this day and every day;
May God's Mother keep you ever
Close beside Her Son, I pray.

SNOW: WRITTEN TO A FRIEND
Mary Wooloughan

It lay so gently on the branches of the tree,
White, so pure,
It seemed to call to you and me,
'Come, share my loveliness.'
We glanced around, each tree did call,
'Come, share our beauty one and all.'

I couldn't help but smile,
Dear Lord, thank you for the bitter cold:
It is worthwhile.

My steps were light as I strolled home.
My spirit soared, and, though alone,
I felt wrapped in love.

The sparkle of the resting snow ·
Gave glimpses of the Lord I know,
A haze of pink lay all around,
As I looked up, the sun shone down.

A silent air, a beauty still,
Snow lay upon the window sill,
A gentle breeze embraced my face,
Each gentle snowflake lay in place.

And as I watched the snowflakes fall,
I couldn't help but then recall,
God had made unique each one –
Like you and me – perfection won.

WORSHIP
Arthur Hurd

A grain of sand to prism the sun,
A flash from the shimmering sea,
Creation's light in the heart of a drop,
An upward look to Thee.

I WALK THE FIELDS
A.J. Holt

I walk the fields I walked in youth
And joys my heart recalls.
How green the grass and meadows
Bright. The memory of it all
Still fills my thoughts with joy
Untold. Although my steps are
Slower now, my spirit still is young.
The joy of youth, the joy of age,
Still fill the thoughts so dear,
And just to know throughout it all,
Dear Lord, You were so near.

FREE TO ALL
Irene Hodgkinson

Have you thought
Of the things you cannot buy,
The golden glow of sunrise,
A brilliant evening sky,
Cobwebs in the hedgerows,
Early morning dew,
The trilling of the early birds
Calling out to you.
The view from the highest hill
When all is peace,
The world is still,
The sound of a tractor
At the end of the day,
The wonderful scent
Of new-mown hay,
Primroses in spring,
Fledglings in the nest,
And autumn colours.
We truly are blessed.
These are things that will always be
For those that love them
Ever free.

THIS NEW DAY
Marilyn Ashcroft

The dawn breaks through with a rosy hue,
The grass is wet with the sparkling dew.
The sunlight glints on the spider's web,
The dewdrops cling to the spider's thread.
A new day dawns all fresh and bright,
The world awakes with the morning light.
Will you give this day to the King of Kings?
Will you serve Him still whate'er it brings?
Look to the Lord at the break of day,
Ask Him to guide you along the way.
Greet the day with a smile and a song,
Spread some cheer as you travel along.
For the Lord has given this day to you,
So seek His glory in all that you do.

THE WAY AHEAD
Gaynor D. Williams

Go forward into morning's grace
With childhood's eager, trusting face.
Explore those castles in the air
While wistful dreams still linger there.
Discard the brooding discontent
With the sorrows of the past.
Embrace each precious day of life
As if it were the last.

PRAISE
Janet Gould

I see You in creation
In every opening flower.
I see You in my children
In every shining hour.
Not just in formal worship
Within a structured shrine;
I praise Your blessed and holy name
In every day that's mine.

THE GREAT REBIRTH
J. Dalmain

We look through winter's window-pane
Into a garden grey and still;
No sign that life will come again,
Thrushes sing or robins trill.
Evening falls dark upon the day,
Resigned, we turn our face away.

Slowly treads spring; so lightly,
Perhaps we're unable to see
Returning life – oh, so quietly,
In the heart of bulb, flower and tree.
Now step outside, feel the soft earth –
God gives to you this great rebirth!

I WONDER WHY?
E.P. Haley

I wonder why the sky is blue,
And why the clouds are grey,
What makes the sun to shed its rays
Through all the summer day.

I wonder why the grass is green,
The buttercup is gold,
What makes the dewdrop fall to earth,
And winter days so cold.

The morning mist on spider's web,
Blackberries ripe and soft,
The busy hum of bumble bee,
And apples in the loft.

So many and so wonderful,
So much to see and learn,
And God Who made the world so fair,
Asks our love in return.

SISTER SPRING
Sister Imelda King

Don't hurry, Sister Spring,
Come slowly,
Keep their trees in their light green,
Stay the daffodils –
Golden smiles
On earth's furrowed face.

No time to admire nature's beauties
If the cherry blossom
Droops and fades ere we've time to say,
'Welcome back again.'

Let the pear trees
Like fairy brides
Keep wearing white
For a longer while.

Butterflies and bees,
Moths on the wing,
Don't need to come just yet.
There's so much to see,
Eyes long to devour,
Drink their fill.

Dear spring, don't hurry,
Come slowly,
Halt the tit's nesting –
We love to see
This acrobat
Hang upside down.

I suspect
His creator
Does too.

How wonderful is He,
The Lord of life,
To have given us you,
Sister Spring,
So
Don't hurry,
Come slowly . . .
Slowly . . .

I THANK THEE, LORD
Muriel Manton

For the gift of a bright new day,
For the children I see at play,
For the rainbow after rain,
For the joy that follows pain,
I thank Thee, Lord.

For the seasons as they pass,
For daisies peeping through the grass,
For roses in the summertime,
For the poets' verse and rhyme,
I thank Thee, Lord.

For springtime when winter's past,
For summer joys fleeting fast,
For autumn's glowing days of gold,
For winter's frost and cold,
I thank Thee, Lord.

STAINED GLASS
Glenda Mitchel Palmer

Only to be His holy window
Stained with the crimson glass of His blood;
Always to show His purple shadow,
The golden glow of His thorny crown.

And then, when set in place,
With the radiance of the sun behind;
Reflecting rainbows, oh, so glorious
Of His love for me, and for Him, mine.

ACCEPTANCE
Michael A. Rouse

I sometimes stop: stand back and look –
Thinking how fortunate am I
That God has given me health and strength,
A love of life and joy in living –
The world seems then a brighter place;
Uplifted thoughts become a prayer.

The greatest joy that I have known
Is knowing that myself I am –
Acceptance now of what I have,
To use more fully all my gifts –
Brings blessings more than untold wealth
And ever wanting something new.

HOLY EUCHARIST:
A THANK YOU
Myra Reeves

Lord,
Most of us are old
And cold.
Because we cannot kneel
We feel
Sadness at the deprivation
Of that symbol of adoration.
Our hands and feet are numb.
Nevertheless we come.
With troubled hearts we raise
Our elder sacrifice of praise.

We receive with bowed head
The holy bread,
And over us the sweet words fall
Of love for all.

We smile at one another,
Sister to sister, brother to brother,
Our warmed souls are at rest,
We, the old, are blest.

DAWN
Eva W. Taylor

The day is breaking, the sky is silently filling
  with light,
While birds are waking, their joyous songs bid
  farewell to the night.
All nature is stirring, the leaves are rustling
  to herald the dawn,
The flowers are lifting their dew-filled heads
  to welcome the morn,
And all of the world with joy is sharing the
  coming of day,
As sun's rays unfurl the clouds, and darkness
  no longer can stay.
Night flies defeated – a new day in glory is born!

FRUITFULNESS
C.J. Gaskin

I walked into the cold dark still of night
Musing on fallen leaves and their life's day,
On chill of death, and spring so far away;
When silently the ground with snow was white.
The stars, so clear before, the moon once bright
Were veiled by glistening falling flakes' display.
But such is cyclic seasons' patterned way
We in next summer's sun will yet delight.
I will love autumn's sun-kissed harvest gold,
And marvel at the Heavens and God's Earth,
And all His creatures fashioned in His mould.
On us You lavish talents from our birth,
Map out our life, and destiny unfold,
While sharing gifts which tell all of Your worth.

MOTHER EARTH
Joan Manning Wesson

I love you, earth,
Your smell,
Your feel,
When I'm planting seeds
Or looking at a field.
The soft, sweet earth
After the snow has gone,
Concealing food for birds
To feed upon.
Roots always endless
And life reborn again,
Ever endless.

THE HAND OF GOD
Marilyn Ashcroft

I see the hand of God above
In all the world around.
From sunlit plain to oceans deep,
From starlit sky to mountain steep.
Wherever you may look on earth
God's handiwork is found.
From flower and field to trees so tall,
From lake and vale to waterfall.
We see God's all-creative power
Expressed in nature's harmony.
From cooling breeze to soft white snow,
From gentle rain to sunset glow.
A world created by God's hand,
Showing perfect artistry.

GOD'S PAINTING
Janet Gould

My children call,
'Come see God's painting!'

Burnt Sienna
Outlines hilltops;
Summer sun
Glows low.
Golden strokes
Blend evening embers,
Erasing afternoon.

'He does good work,'
They smile.

I THANK YOU, LORD
Thomas Foy

I thank You for Your goodness, Lord,
In all the years gone by.
Through all my joys and sorrows
Your help was always nigh.
I thank You for the friends sincere
I've met on life's highway.
I thank You for the rising sun
That gladdens each new day.
I thank You for the soft south winds
That sing among the trees,
They tell of fruitful harvest times
And shimmering summer seas.
I thank You for the stars that shine
To brighten each long night.
True signs of Your unceasing care,
Great Lord of power and might.

GRANDSON
William Giles

There is a sunbeam in my life,
That shines all day,
And shines all night,
And scatters starlight in my heart,
And fills my striving soul with light.

The balm of Heaven in his kiss,
Eternal beauty in his smile,
He has come from halls of bliss,
And in that love-filled paradise
His spirit lingers yet awhile.

He reaches up with trusting hand
For me to guide his shaky step;
Yet I it is who need his help
To lead me to the promised land.

He has a magic year or two,
Before his body traps his mind,
And binds it with demanding flesh,
And wraps it in the complex mesh
Of all the things men fill their lives with.

And I am near the end of the road
That leads to where he's come from;
And I needed to be reassured,
And shown the living love of God.

But when I see each joyous step
And the radiant beauty of his smile.
I know that God is with me yet,
And with me
To the end of time.

IN HARMONY
Gaynor D. Williams

Alone
By the firelight,
Not asleep, just drifting
In time with music and voices
Haunting.
Old songs
Half forgotten,
Misty faces mingle,
Fragile blossoms of memory
Bloom still.

TO THE ROBIN
Meryl Tookaram

Thank you for the notes of beauty
That you bring to my modern, noisy
Day, for the cheerful chatter,
That never fails to make me smile
When life seems grey.
But most of all, robin,
For those sad notes. They
Make me pause for thought
While on my hurried way,
And in doing so
Give thanks to God for
Yet another day.

AT THE END OF THE DAY
Irene Hodgkinson

It's a wonderful feeling
To look to the skies
At the stars that are twinkling
At the moon sailing by.
There's such a feeling
Of peace and content
When work is done,
When your energy's spent,
When at last you realise
The glory and wonder of the skies.
You go inside and shut the door,
But it's a memory you'll have for evermore.

NOT JUST YET
Richard Merry

My holiday on earth must end one day.
Thoughts of returning home bring no regret.
But, loth to leave the golden sands, I pray . . .
Please – not just yet.

Some day the skies must gather me: but now
The sun still shines as through an endless June.
And, though pale autumn's fruit
   must leave the bough . . .
Please – not too soon.

The debt still owed; the unaccomplished task;
And, still unfaced,
   the challenge that grows stronger –
These things are my arrears. I simply ask . . .
A little longer.

Then, duty over, give me space to run
Among the million joys still left untried –
The sights, the sounds, the tastes.
   Please let my fun
Be satisfied.

Expand the fleeting hour, which age contracts
To some derisory moment quickly spent.
My tree of life still blossoms. Let the axe
Pause and relent.

With lengthened hours
   and days beyond my due,
I'll still have yearnings when I take my bow.
Yet I shall warmly greet that final cue . . .
But not just now.

THE LIGHT OF THE WORLD
Lyn Bevan

The light of the world is everywhere,
It's in a blade of grass,
It's in the sunset over a stile,
It's in a baby's smile,
So look for it wherever you are,
And it will fill your life,
Lifting you up to pastures new,
Making your life worthwhile.

THE SILVER SEA
Marilyn Ashcroft

To sit and watch the sun
  set upon a silver sea,
Is a moment that's filled with beauty
  and deep tranquillity.
It's a time for recollection
  and thoughts you can't explain,
But a sense of peace and happiness
  floods your soul again,
For a moment such as this
  is precious beyond measure.
The assurance which it brings
  is something you can treasure.
There are times which speak at depth
  of the wonders of our Lord,
Of the joy and peace of His love
  that's into our lives outpoured.

Designed and produced by
Genesis Productions Limited
30 Great Portland Street
London W1N 5AD

First published in Great Britain in 1986 by
Century Hutchinson Ltd
Brookmount House, 62-65 Chandos Place,
London WC2N 4NW

Century Hutchinson Publishing Group (Australia) Pty Ltd
16-22 Church Street, Hawthorn, Melbourne, Victoria 3122

Century Hutchinson Group (NZ) Ltd
32-34 View Road, PO Box 40-086, Glenfield, Auckland 10

Century Hutchinson Group (SA) Pty Ltd
PO Box 337, Bergvlei 2012, South Africa

Designed by Bernard Higton
Printed and bound in the Netherlands by
Drukerij Giethoorn, Meppel

British Library Cataloguing in Publication Data
From the heart: poems of praise and thanks.
–(Treasuries of inspiration; 3)
1. English poetry   2. Gratitude in literature   3. Christian life in literature
I Series
821'.008'0353   PR1195.G7

ISBN 0-7126-1404-4